CHRISTMAS GIFT!

CHR

ISTMAS GIFT!

FERROL SAMS

LONGSTREET PRESS
Atlanta, Georgia

Published by
LONGSTREET PRESS, INC.
2150 Newmarket Parkway
Suite 102
Marietta, Georgia 30067

Printed in the United States of America

1st printing, 1989

Library of Congress Catalog Number 89-084528

ISBN 0-929264-59-2

This book was printed by R. R. Donnelley and Sons, Crawfordsville, Indiana.
The text type was set in Goudy Old Style by Typo-Repro Service, Inc., Atlanta,
Georgia. Design by Paulette Lambert.

To

Helen

For her grandchildren

CHRISTMAS GIFT!

This was the best Christmas we ever had. It had to be because it always is. I heard my mother say so every year. It was she who protested that she didn't want a present; she just wanted us all to be together and to love one another. It was she who feared that seasonal frenzy would overshadow eternal verities. She was apprehensive that we might get so caught up in the excitement of giving and, regardless of what anyone tried to teach us, of getting, that we would ignore "the true meaning of Christmas."

She would have loved this one. Last year the family was broke and we said, "Let's don't give any presents." Then we dipped into reserves and gave them anyway. This year even the reserves were gone. There was still, however, the thrill in the heart, the building excitement, the rush of preparation. There was still the awareness of hope, the weary world rejoicing. I felt it; I watched it; I pondered. Many people nowadays say that Christmas is for children, thus appearing a little world-weary, skeptical of a new and glorious morn, forgetful that joy itself is primitive. Perhaps they have misplaced their sense of wonder and can no longer experience awe; but they are right — Christmas is for children.

This was the Christmas that I set aside grief. I could

not have done it without children. I did not this year forget my parents, my grandparents, my aunts and uncles, my brothers-in-law, all of whom have died; but I gave up mourning for them. I still have more on this side of the Jordan than on the other because friends and family keep multiplying, and they are a great blessing. Only scant years ago I did not regard myself as a marrying man and now, irrespective of feelings of inadequacy, I am a patriarch. My memories cover six decades, and I am again a little child at Christmas.

The grandchildren have given me this. This was the year that I bribed five-year-old Sara Kate to say "Heehaw" in the Christmas pageant. I offered her five dollars, but she held out for seven. Her mother wanted her to be an angel, primarily because that costume is easier to make, but Sara Kate willfully insisted on being a donkey and her mother indulged her. She very nearly indulged me when the heehaw broke loose in the church.

This was the the year that two-year-old Megan exchanged saying "Merry Christmas" for the ebullient, rambunctious "Christmas gift." This was the year that thirteen-year-old Jennifer, our first child of divorce, said, "Thank you, Sambi, for caring about me. This is where I belong."

This was the year that little Helen, shyly approaching her teens, put her arms around my neck spontaneously and said, "I love you." It was the year that Miss Margaret, a pragmatist at age five, listened in Sunday school to a local version of the travail of Christmas — no room at the inn, birth in a stable, cradling in an animal trough, no clothes for a newborn — and, being able to endure it no longer, comfortingly assured her class, "That's all right. He's going to die anyhow."

This was the year that brothers Bo and Barclay did not fight a single time for a whole day. William Joseph, our blessed Down's child, at age six proudly and accurately delivered presents at Aunt Sara's tree. And this was the year that Jimbo and Fletch went to the cemetery with me.

They are my grandchildren and they made Christmas for me. I would like to make one for all of them. I can remember their parents as children, their great-aunts when they were children. I remember their great-grandparents and their great-great-grandparents. I have sixty-six years of Christmas past within me. I will give it to them, for Jennifer is right. This is where they all belong.

Our family is lucky. People speak and write about "sense of place," but ours is visible, tangible. It is the house, and the house still stands. In a hundred and fifty years it has survived the Civil War, carpetbaggers, boll weevils, and the Great Depression. For a while at least, it is safe even from the sucking cusps on that blindly groping tentacle of progress, the powerful sprawl known as Atlanta. The holdings around it have shrunk, divided through legacy and gift until the map of the land has become a jig-saw puzzle, its dividing lines known only to intimates. All of the pieces are still in the family, however, and all of the pieces dovetail and fit. So do the members of the family; my sisters, my nieces and nephews, my children.

In the middle of the puzzle sits the house. Serene and secure, it shelters its sixth generation. Its appearance has been altered by every owner it has had, but the heart of it is unchanged. For a while after my parents died, it drooped, it was sad, but now there are once again little children there. They race resoundingly across the wooden floors, upstairs and downstairs; they laugh, they cry, they sing, they hurt, they grow; the house is happy again. It broods and hovers them under protective wings like fledgling chicks. At times, it almost clucks. Happiness is not a place, but in memory it is frequently identified with one. Our family is not only lucky, it is blessed.

Miss Sis and Mr. Jim were my grandparents. We called them Mammy and Pa. We lived with them in the house, my parents, my three sisters, my aunt and her husband. Mammy's father had built the house and until she died it was hers. At Christmas, Mammy and Pa's other children all came. Two of them lived away off in Atlanta and Jackson and on Christmas Eve they had to spend the night, making eight more people who slept there. The pallets the grownups made of quilts and put on the floor for us children weren't too bad; we were so excited we hardly slept anyway. We kept waking up wondering if Santa Claus had come. I always slept with my older cousin, Pete Giles, and that was not a bad arrangement. Pete and I were going to fight wherever we were anyhow, awake or asleep, and the pallets were as good a place as any.

"Quit kicking."

"I'm not kicking. I'm just turning over."

"You are too kicking."

"No I'm not."

"Yes you are. Here, I'll show you some real kicking."

5

Christmas Eve nights were more demanding of communal consideration before my daddy got a Delco system, put a pump in the well, and built a bathroom at the end of the upstairs hall on the back porch roof. Slop jars were an abomination at any time, but when a cousin who was a comparative stranger in the house turned one over in the middle of the night, it was a catastrophe. It was also a catastrophe if I slept too hard and wet the bed on Pete. Big families teach us to endure much, suffer more, and hold our heads up anyhow. In public, at least.

Getting ready for Christmas was the most organized activity of the year in those rural times. The entire family became involved, and it made getting ready for company seem a minor project, although that, too, was an integral part of it. Not only did it demand a lot of thought, of planning ahead; it impelled prodigious activity and work. As Fayette County, Georgia, was tilted ever so gradually farther and farther away from the sun, the days shortened and our pace on the farm quickened; we had less time to do everything. First light for milking came later each morning and then, before the cows' bags had time to engorge fully, it was all to be done over again in the crisp, fast-falling dusk of the afternoon. There was no farmyard dawdling in December; the temperature dropped quickly in those bob-tailed days and we kept up with it. Stove wood was carried in near run from the woodlot to the big box behind the kitchen stove. The handful of daylight we had was packed: killing hogs, feeding mules, hilling sweet potatoes, taking scuttles of coal to the fireplaces, carrying Mammy's potted plants to the flower pit.

"Make haste before dark catches you, Son."

We made haste about everything, the hours themselves grew faster as the mid-point between autumnal and vernal equinox came closer and closer. Then the ladies of the family and the community crammed into their schedules the added excitement of cooking and baking and preparing seasonal delicacies. They obviously enjoyed it and their attitude increased the peaking anticipation in us children.

"Are you about ready for Christmas?"

"Lawsy mercy, no! Only two cakes done and not enough daylight to turn around."

Auntie was the cake-maker in the family. Her name was Sara Mary, but her parents and brothers called her "Sack." They are all dead now and unavailable for explanation, and I never thought to ask the derivation of that nickname. The children called her "Auntie." She made the fruitcake first and she always liked to have that one, with its richness of nuts and citron and pineapple and cherries and raisins, out of the way well before Thanksgiving so that it would season. She kept it stored in a tightly lidded lard can and twice a week would douse it with blackberry wine. This was wine that she had made herself, and for a teetotaling Baptist she was inordinately proud of it. She always lowered her voice to a conspiratorial level when she spoke of it and with straight spine and stiff neck avowed that people who knew about such things would pronounce her product as good as, if not better than, the finest vintages from France. Who such a connoisseur would have been in our community was a mystery; I knew no one except World War I veterans who had ever tasted French wine. Auntie never served hers to anyone except female kin afflicted with mysteriously periodic abdominal pain. This was a practice that, to the casual observer, validated her assertion that the wine was only for medicinal purposes. I watched carefully, however, and she sloshed more wine on the fruitcake every year than ever soothed the cramps of our entire family of females.

That lard can was the most fragrant one in Georgia, and by Christmas day the cake weighed considerably more than when it came from the oven. It had the spicy, fruitful aroma of foreign lands, of forbidden nectar, and

Auntie could slice it so thin that the light glowed through the cherries and pineapple and citron as beautifully as through medieval stained glass. Her fruitcake was not pleasant on a child's tongue, but it had authority. It was a tradition of which I was afraid not to partake for fear it would not be proffered again, and always by next year I might have learned to like it.

The first cake to be made after Thanksgiving was the amalgamation. Auntie said it kept very well and could be got out of the way before the real rush set in. It was a layered cake with a filling of fresh coconut, raisins, and this year's pecans, all held together with a little sugar syrup. The batter was important. We had a big and very worn mixing bowl, its honey-colored porcelain glaze veined by tiny little lines that never quite became cracks, its status ensured by the fact that it had been a wedding present to my grandparents, its continued presence endorsement of Auntie's proclamation that if you take care of things they last forever.

She did not use any utensils other than the bowl in making her batter. With her hands she squeezed the butter and sugar together, the mixture crawling and squirting from between her fingers in thin ribbons that fell back upon themselves and were squeezed again. The eggs and flour and milk were added, and then Auntie came into her own. She sat in a low, cane-bottomed chair, the back legs of which had been worn considerably shorter than the front ones through generations of relaxed tilting, and took Mammy's mixing bowl into her lap. I realize now that she did this so that she could grip the bowl between her thighs and steady it, but as a child it never occurred to me that Auntie had thighs, let alone that she might grip anything between them.

She stirred and stirred the batter with her hands. Then she began an over-and-over motion with those hands, similar to that of the paddle wheel on a steamboat. The cake batter cooperated. There developed a rhythm and a sound not unlike a heavy horse clopping over a wooden bridge. The pace quickened, became a gallop, a lighter-footed horse. The hands became a blur, the cake batter a creamy golden flood folding and whirling upon itself in constantly shifting patterns.

"You have to keep your wrists just a little limp, but not floppy." The motion and the noise went on and on. This was why Auntie's cakes were lighter and fluffier, she explained, than either my mother's or my grandmother's. "Nobody can beat a cake better than I can — if I do say so myself."

The neck was not as stiff as when she talked of her wine, but the tone was just as confidential. We children knew better than to repeat it. No need to disrupt higher feminine serenity.

"I declare, sometimes you can rattle like your tongue is tied in the middle and loose at both ends."

As soon as she poured the rich mixture into the baking pans, she made us wash our hands and placed the bowl carefully on the floor. We squatted around it, surreptitiously yanking the bowl away from each other and back again. We popped batter-laden fingers in and out of our mouths as hastily as possible, heedless of the slurping noise we made; competition for Auntie's batter was keen. "Here, now! You break my grandma's cake bowl and I won't bother with telling Santa; I'll just warm your little settees myself this very minute."

The cake was baked in what she called a moderate oven. There was no thermometer on that wood-burner; Auntie slipped broom straws in and out to tell when the cake was done. Woe betide any youngun who ran through the stove-room with jarring tread and raised the threat of making the cake fall. Santa Claus would certainly be told about that; he was already making his list, you know. Baby Jesus was not mentioned. The children loved Him, to be sure, but the rewards of being good to win the favors of Santa Claus were much more immediate. The dictum may be infallible that it is more blessed to give than to receive, but I wonder. Who has watched the eyes of someone who did not receive? We tiptoed through that kitchen when Auntie was baking. A month before Christmas she could have controlled a whole orphanage of children single-handedly. The cakes, sacrosanct and inviolable, awaited the big day on the sideboard or high on kitchen shelves, well beyond our reach.

As important as the cooking, as the cakes, was the Christmas tree. Wreaths were fashioned and hung on doors, mistletoe suspended from lintels, garlands of evergreen entwined in the stair railing in the hall, but the tree was the focus of decoration. Although we needed a lot of help with it, we children were made to feel that it was ours, from procuring it to adorning it. We always wanted to put it up early; our mother tried to delay us as nearly as possible until a week before Christmas.

"It'll dry out and needles will be all over the parlor. It might even catch fire."

When she could withstand our pleas no longer, we went and got the tree. Before we were big enough to walk the fields and woods with adequate stride, Pa Jim would harness Clyde and Pet to the wagon and carry us to the back side of The Place to cut it. Most people said "farm." Occasionally Pa Jim would revert and say "the whole plantation," but I had the feeling he had abandoned that word after the yankees came and the slaves were gone. Most of the time, he said "The Place," and that was good enough for me. We were bundled into so much limb-splinting clothing against the cold that it was not altogether bone-jarring to sit flat in the jolting bed of the wagon, but it gave a shimmer to one's vision. Mr. Jim would yell at you if you stood up and held the side. The wheel might hit a rock and fling you out of the wagon on your head like it did Willie Hugh Braxton when he was a little boy. Cuddin Willie didn't die, but he lay unconscious with brain fever three weeks and never had been right; all his children were smarter than he was. He married a Whitcomb and the good Lord above knew that didn't put a dab of brains in the line; so if he hadn't stood up in the wagon, no telling what he might have amounted to. Besides, if we didn't sit down Santa Claus was sure to find out that we hadn't been minding. It was worse to disobey a grandparent than a parent. We sat.

Pa Jim would tie the mules in a cedar grove and lift us out of the wagon one at a time, and we would struggle through briers and winter brown weeds in selection of our tree. His was the final decision but he was a master arbitrator and first listened indulgently to all opinions. The sharp, somehow ancient, smell of the cedars mingled with the spice of rabbit tobacco and the sun-baked flatness of broom sedge and gave us all enough aromatic recall to last for Christmases to come. We would gasp in delighted startle if a covey of quail happened to erupt, and we would squat down to inspect neat little mounds of rabbit pills, all secret and cozy at the base of a grass hummock, but the main purpose of our foray was the tree. It had to be just right. The parlor had a fourteen-foot ceiling and the tree had to be tall, skinny, and yet bushy. When the practiced eye of my grandfather finally found the one that would do for that year, we were all ordered to stand back while he took the axe to it. Then he shouldered it and we trailed him back to the wagon.

The trip home was wonderful. We children were scattered among the bouncing branches of the tree like so many bundled-up birds and the wagon rode smoother, the excitement of procurement intensified by the fragrance of the boughs, the prickling of the cedar against exposed skin of only negligible attention. One year there was an abandoned bird nest anchored in the tree and my sisters cautioned me to protect it as an unexpected ornament. It added a sense of mystery.

While Pa Jim unhitched the mules, Comp, who was Auntie's husband, went to work to mount the tree. It had to stand upright, perfectly straight; it could not lean even the least bit. We always happened to have an old lard crate and he would try that first, nailing it to the base and then filling it with rocks. It never worked. He would lug the tree into the parlor, having carefully removed all lamps and breakable items from its path. The tree would lap over at the ceiling. "About a foot or a foot and a half," he would murmur as if to himself and whistle softly under his breath; not any tune, just plain whistling. Then he'd haul the tree back to the yard and cut some more off. Another trip back into the house caused enough skinning of branches against door jambs to add the spice of resin to the air.

It usually took at least a third trip in and out and back in to the parlor every year before Comp turned red, uttered strange Tennessee sounds under his breath, and knocked the lard crate off the bottom of the tree. Then it took at least an hour for him to hunt up some old two-by-fours, straighten some used nails, and construct a proper base and sufficiently sturdy mount for our Christmas tree. During this hour we children were almost as quiet as when Auntie had a cake in the oven. Sensitive to adult moods, we felt the urge to tiptoe even outdoors. Comp most likely would have been frustrated trying to control an orphanage of children, but they could have made him think he was good at it. He had his own charisma; he mentioned neither Santa Claus nor Baby Jesus.

After Pa Jim went off to Atlanta and got his operation and became feeble, Comp was the one who went with us to get our tree, but it was different. For one thing we were older and longer-legged and we walked. It was an exhausting trek, for the prettiest cedars invariably grew on the back side of The Place. Sometimes we could not find one that was perfect in size and shape and Comp would chop the top from a larger tree, a process that was somehow almost as demeaning as leaving a half-dressed carcass in the woods and not nearly so magic as finding a tree standing in solitary and pristine perfection, exactly right for that particular year. If we complained about the distance or mentioned fatigue, Comp would mutter that the exercise was good for us.

"You need to burn off some of that infernal nervous energy so you'll go to bed early and sleep good tonight."

I was grown before it occurred to me that Comp, who had been reared in the heart of Knoxville, had not the faintest idea how to harness a pair of mules to a wagon and that he nurtured a grave distrust of any animal that weighed more than he. Also he had been an old bachelor when he married Auntie, a settled-into-routine, neat and orderly, military man. He had a monthly retirement check even through the Depression and was frequently invited to make loans within the family, a situation he learned to sidestep with some dexterity. If he was a little grumpier than usual through Christmas, we overlooked it in the joy of the season and always thanked him profusely for helping us with the tree.

There is nothing that can so suddenly darken a room and fill it with enchantment as putting a thickly branched cedar in the corner. The room, even with its familiar furniture, the same pictures on the wall, was transformed into a grotto of incredible mystery. The tree perfumed the whole downstairs and anticipation reached a new peak. There has seldom been any project to match the way we dressed and adorned it. We hung it with strings of popcorn and cranberries. We looped garlands of multi-colored paper chains around it. We attached to its branches sweetgum and sycamore balls covered with tin-foil that we had carefully peeled from the paper in Pa Jim's Sir Walter Raleigh tobacco tins.

Mammy unlocked her closet, that sacrosanct reliquary forbidden to all her children and grandchildren, and brought down the Box of Ornaments. There were age-softened ropes of tinsel, tarnished by time and somewhat moth-eaten from the yearly handling by excited children. There were colored pictures of angels on heavy paper and brightly colored turn-of-the-century girls with the wings of cherubs framing and crowding their portraits. We hung them on the tree first. There were glittering spun-glass balls, some of them with hand-blown indented sun-sets or delicate spines, some tapered to points on both ends, some suspended within individual frames of tinsel. They were red and green and gold and blue and silver, and they were handed down from distant days when the family could afford such symbols of luxury. To us they were jewels, as rich in color as the accessories bedecking an imperious medieval queen but more fragile than egg shells. No matter that the color was scaling off or that there was a hole in the back of more than an occasional one. With reverence we unrolled them from their tissue paper, itself a little yellowed with age and so wrinkled from repeated use that it was soft as mole skin. Despite the care with which we handled them and hung them on the tree, their number thinned each year. A jostling elbow or an inadvertent brush against a suspending twig could send one of those gorgeous balls to crash upon the hardwood floor in shimmering fragments, a thousand tiny mirrors of our dismay.

The last ornament to go on the tree was the bird. Wondrously wrought, it had been colored red and white and green when new but was now mostly silver, its eyes worn smooth and sightless. Its little glass legs ended in points within balancing springs mounted on a rusted candle clip so that it swayed and trembled on the limb where we fastened it. It had the general configuration and noble proportions of a brown thrasher and was a Yuletide icon. Its long tail was made of the same kind of hair that was in our grandfather's shaving brush, and over the years that tail had become loosened. If the bird tilted the least bit forward, the entire tail disappeared into the body cavity so that the creature resembled a violated wren; consequently we were careful to perch him so that his head was raised to the ceiling as if triumphant in song and the splendid sweep of his tail was clearly visible. We learned early not to quarrel about who had the privilege of placing the bird on the tree. There was ample time to sneak alone into the room and change the position to suit oneself. Often that bird was moved a dozen times or more before Christmas Day, with never a voice raised in acrimony and with neither Baby Jesus dismayed nor Santa Claus one whit the wiser. The grownups said we were sweet while trimming the tree.

The foil icicles were last to go on. There was a flat cardboard box of them plucked from previous Christmas trees, but they were twisted and crumpled, their use requiring patience and care. Except in the very leanest years, our indulgent mother always bought two new packs folded straight in regimented rows. They were a delight to distribute, but we had to use the old ones first, to honor the gospel by Auntie and Mammy of "Waste not, want not." Sara and Janice and Jimmie draped the icicles one by one in rank and row on each individual limb. I was impatient and believed in tossing a hank of them toward the top of the tree and letting them fall in haphazard glitter where they might. I was usually excused from icicle duty; my sisters wanted that tree to be perfect. It always was.

We had no electric lights. In the daytime, light through the windows reflected from the balls and tinsel with the chilling wink of winter. Night was the real time of the tree. That was when it lived completely within the room. For the week before Christmas, we were allowed to build a fire in the parlor grate every night and at least knock the chill of refrigeration off the tall old room. The fire sheen brought the tree to life. Dressed in our footed pajamas with flaps in the seats, we watched the kaleidoscope of color dance through and over the somber mystery of cedar in such flicker and twinkle that we were bemused. The colors were richer because they were muted, and the mystery of Christmas filled our hearts. We understood little, but we sensed a great deal. When I was a little boy, every Christmas tree was perfect. Regardless of where the bird was perched.

To be complete, the Christmas tree had to be almost smothered in packages. Wrapping them was fun but purchasing the gifts was even better. This activity came under the purview of one person and one person only as far as we were concerned. Miss Mildred was our mother. Her in-laws called her "Millen," and all of them loved her as much as she loved them. She was the one who took us Christmas shopping and there was none of that sterile, preplanned, mind-made-up-ahead-of-time gift selection for her. We shopped. Some time in the week before Christmas she bundled us all into her square Chevrolet with quilts to wrap around our legs against the cold, and we careened merrily off to Atlanta. If it was bitterly cold, Pa Jim heated bricks on the hearth and gave all the children one as a foot warmer. Each of us clutched what money we had earned and our Christmas lists. We knew for whom we were going to buy, and how much we could afford to spend, but had not the faintest idea what we were going to purchase. This added to the excitement, the frenzy, the urgency.

The sidewalks of Atlanta were full of jostling, rushing shoppers, the throng dividing and closing again around the Salvation Army people stationed before the entrance to every major store. Neat and clean, their hair in prim buns on their necks, the Salvation Army lassies rang their hand bells all day long over little cauldrons suspended from tripods, shifting from one foot to the other to stay warmer. They wore no makeup and they needed none.

Their breaths made white puffs in the air and that air in turn reddened their faces, brought tears to their eyes, and made their noses leak. We regarded them as Protestant nuns; they certainly looked as though they were bound by the same vows.

Standing in the cold before Rich's and Davison's and Sears Roebuck there was usually also a Salvation Army ensemble, and it somehow did not seem incongruous to hear "Silent Night" blaring down the corridors of White-hall Street on the notes of trumpet, cornet, and trombone. It mingled with the cacophony of automobile horns and police whistles and added up to Christmas in the City. Our first stop of the day was always a Salvation Army station where we tossed coins into the kettle under the supervising eye of Miss Mildred and earned the smiling "God bless you" from the bell ringers. None of us will ever hear "the true meaning of Christmas" without eventually envisioning red-trimmed black bonnets that framed parted-in-the-middle widow's peaks and chaste, chapped faces. We will also hear the constant rapid tinkle of those imploring bells. The sound impels us to give, to share.

The shopping was exhilarating. The choices one had for a quarter in those days were unbelievable. The clerks at Kress's chewed gum and said from just behind their teeth, "Kin I hep you?" The ladies at Rich's wore black dresses with white collars, and spoke flutingly from the back of their throats, "Is someone waiting on you?" At both places we learned that it was all right to say, "No'm, I'm just looking."

Pa Jim always said a fool and his money are soon parted, and for the kind of extravagance we were practicing we were not about to be rushed into unwise selections. Scarves for Pa Jim and Comp were available for twenty-five cents; so were boxes of four linen handkerchiefs embroidered in Switzerland with little knotted-up rosebuds for Mammy and Auntie. The same price range enabled me to select treasures for my sisters: a china swan for Jimmie Kate, who was older than I, had a room to herself, and her own little roll-top desk. She never sat at the desk, but it was an off-limits repository for her treasured bric-a-brac. I could get a marvelous crystal ball for Janice with a tiny snowman in it that would be swirled over with white flakes when the ball was inverted. Sara was the baby and would love the little Betty Boop china doll that really closed its eyes when horizontal. "Yes, ma'am, you can help me now, please."

The cousins drew names every year, and by some fluke that I did not at the time connect with the maneuvering of mothers, Pete and I usually had each other's name. He lived in Atlanta and always told me within thirty seconds of unwrapping his gift precisely how much I had paid for it, even the year I bought the sack of marbles at Woolworth's and wrapped them in a Rich's box. At least I knew better than to succumb to the economic enticement of any article that was "Made in Japan." We may have been country children but we recognized that slogan as the epitome of cheapness and flimsiness. I cannot for the life of me recall any gift Pete ever gave me, although he did so habitually. If there arise doubt that it is more blessed to give than to receive, one has to concede that it is certainly more memorable. That is an entirely different philosophy and not nearly so noble.

The gifts we purchased for Miss Mildred had to be acquired on a skulking foray with frequent over-the-shoulder watchfulness, for she was constantly present. Each year she proclaimed that she wanted no gift; she just wanted us all to be together in love and to remember the true spirit of Christmas. She refused to give any hint of preference and this consequently made her the recipient of gaudy scarves, cheap perfume, or plastic trinkets that damned the taste of her spawn but evoked paeans of approbation from her. She frequently reminded us in our shopping that it is the thought that counts, but I cringe when I remember some of my gifts to her. Even a child should have been able to muster better thoughts.

We pooled our resources to buy a gift for our father. He was by no stretch of imagination a Kress's man, and for him we dauntlessly invaded Rich's or even Davison-Paxon's, the other fancy store farther up town, and spent far more on his gift than on anyone else's. With excitement we selected a genuine leather belt or an expensive tie or even, in one affluent year, a pair of soft leather gloves lined with the downy richness of rabbit fur that cost us right at five dollars. Miss Mildred was always at our elbows with beaming hints when we shopped for Daddy.

For my grandfather, I bought the same thing every year. He was such a favored friend that I had absolutely no doubt at all what he liked or how to please him; he got a pound box of chocolate-covered cherries. Mr. Jim had a sweet tooth and, in addition, a proclivity for sharing with a grandchild anything he had that was suitable. Those cherries cost a quarter, no matter where you bought them. They were available in Fayetteville at the drug store; so there was no use to lug them all over Atlanta. I always felt clumsy with a laden shopping bag sidling in and out of bronze-fronted elevators queened by black women in green uniforms. They perched on a stool in the corner and measured off the crowds with a stick before rattling the doors closed. They spoke with more proper enunciation than anyone I knew except school teachers.

"Third floor. Ladies' ready-to-wear, foundation garments, lingerie, and hosiery. Watch your step, please."

Oh, watch your step indeed! Downtown Atlanta was so full of thrills at Christmastime that a child from the country had the urge to skip. So was the farm. Christmas was a skipping time, no matter where you were.

Our daddy was imbued with every masculine virtue that has ever been delineated, albeit he was infested also with a leavening share of masculine vices. Nowhere has there ever lived an adult who enjoyed Christmas more than he. If our mother represented the Book and candle, he was holly and mistletoe. He believed in Baby Jesus but somewhere deep within his pool of genes lurked hamadryads and druids and oak forests, and in December every year they surfaced just enough to flash a silvery sheen into our eyes and let us know they were there.

After all, they were older than Advent; they would not be forever denied. Further, were not both religions based ultimately on human sacrifice? Miss Margaret is right. Not to worry.

To us, our father represented the true spirit of Christmas as much as our mother; the disparity in their interpretations added nothing but enrichment. He approached the day with abandon, and revelry was his strong suit. Profligacy and extravagance could be condoned just this once; so long, of course, as you did not go into actual debt.

In no area was his patrimony exemplified more than in our Christmas turkey. No matter how severe the Depression, how near depletion the cash reserves, how many of our neighbors might be eating less exotic fare, we had a turkey. This was in direct contradiction of Mr. Jim's maxim, "If you don't raise it, you don't eat it." We had no turkeys on our farm and every year our father bought one. With cash money. A couple of times Miss Sis had procured a setting of eggs and tried to raise turkeys but had abandoned the project in disgust. They were stupid fowl, she said, and the young ones would not stay under cover when it rained, preferring to stand exposed and stretch their necks straight up with mouths agape until they drowned. I never witnessed this but Miss Sis proclaimed it and Mr. Jim affirmed it; so it had to be true.

Where our daddy procured the turkey we never knew for sure. He refused to give direct answers to the questions either of where he got something or where he had been. He was wont to quote Mr. Ben Hightower when Mr. Hollingsworth asked him where he had managed to find a particularly delectable gallon of white whiskey.

"If you like that likker, Holly, then by God drink it."

This attitude extended to the acquisition of the Christmas turkey, and we children rapidly learned not to ask. Our mother never learned. She never quit asking, but she never got any other answer.

The turkey was a wonder. It was always a gobbler, brought home in a coarse croker sack that had a hole cut out from which its head protruded. In addition to this precaution, its legs were tied with binder twine. It lay quietly in the back of our father's car while a suitable coop was fashioned for it. It was a mammoth fowl. The head was huge, covered with slick skin like humans get from burns and colored bright red and azure blue, a most improbable apparition. There was a snout that hung down across its beak, and fiery wattles that dangled and quivered like Cuddin Addie's tier of receding chins when she made announcements in Sunday school. It was always a little disconcerting to me when the sack was removed to reveal feathers on that bird. The scales and plates of a dinosaur would have been more appropriate.

The monster had to be confined and force fed on corn for at least two weeks, not only to fatten it but to "clean it out." It had been raised we knew not where, pecking in strange barnyard and behind unknown privy.

"If you like that turkey, eat it."

Only at this season our farm rang to its throaty, trumpeting call, the repetition louder and more insistent the colder the day and the nearer Christmas. It added to the crescendo that kept building toward Baby Jesus and Santa Claus, and thereby contributed unknowingly to the true meaning of Christmas.

The grandparents fed the turkey and the grandchildren tagged along in wonder. This was not one of Miss Sis's worn-out layers, pale-combed and listless with senility, being prepared for Sunday dinner and cowering in a corner at our approach. This puffed-out, strutting, big-chested import, whose snout incomprehensibly grew longer and redder when he fluffed out his feathers, challenged our presence; his wingtips made scraping sounds in the dust while his pinions squeaked like shifting timbers. He was the Pentecostal Lamb, the fatted calf. The prodigals were returning in force to home haven and they would be welcomed with feasting.

The first year I can remember the turkey is the year I learned never to become personally attached to one. This exotic guest, bedecked and bedizened in plumage strange and iridescent in the sunlight of our barnyard, arrogant, imperious, altogether noble, after weeks of daily homage from me, was lugged to the woodpile very early on the morning of December 23 by Comp and Mr. Jim. It took both of them. There was no fanfare; the neck was simply stretched across the chopping block and the axe glinted as it rose. Then it fell with efficient, unceremonious "chunk," and that was the end of the foreign prince. The severed head lay with glazing eyes and slowly gaping beak against the woodpile. With twin geysers of crimson spurting and spattering from his stump of a neck, the body of the prince erupted with prodigious unguided leaps into the abandoned, awkward dance of death. Then it collapsed into a twitching mountain of feathers, nothing more than meat for the table. My ears rang. The sky whirled. "The lone and level sands stretched far away."

I was accustomed to my mother killing and dressing a frying-size chicken. She wrung and snapped the neck with strong circular wrist motion and, when the bird had stopped flopping and quivering, carried the limber carcass into the stove room. She immersed it immediately in boiling water and then rapidly plucked the sodden feathers and wrapped them in newspaper to be burned later around the washpot.

"Wait till tomorrow to burn those chicken feathers, Millen. The wind's in the east today."

The turkey was different. It was picked dry. It took both Auntie and Mother to do it and it took forever. Comp helped. The larger, softer feathers were stuffed into a sack to be tied later around sticks for dusters; the ends of the wings, stiff-feathered and curved, were cut off and used as whisks for stove and table top and hearth. Our father disdained any gobbler that weighed less than forty or fifty pounds, and it was labor to lift the carcass over open flames to singe it. For some of the embedded pin feathers, Comp had to use the pliers. When he was done the skin was cratered and pocked and pimpled in compelling pattern and texture.

The heart, the liver, the gizzard were removed and cooked separately as the base for giblet gravy. The gizzard was wondrous. Bigger than a man's fist, colored brown and red with purple and silvery white streaks, molded into mounds as tightly packed as a hoarded purse, it was an arcane treasure. I was big-eyed when I first saw Mother pluck one in triumph from the turkey's cavity with blindly grappling hand. She expertly slit the muscular wall, taking care to remove the sac of contents without opening it, and exposed the bleached and bloodless lining, as ridged and deeply grooved as coarse-grained corduroy or the bark on a very old sourwood tree. The foreign prince, that wondrous fowl, had lived for himself in transient glory, but he had died for me. He was so big they could not fit him into the roaster and had to cook him in a lard can on top of the stove. So be it.

The aroma of the bird cooking in the stove room mingled with the fragrance of the tree in the parlor and became the foundation for the perfumes of Christmas. There were other tantalizing ingredients, and I always include the fragrance of fresh coconut, faint, but rich and heavy-bodied. Looking back, I am conscious of the benevolence of the grownups in our house. They made us feel important. They assigned chores to all of the children, often tasks they could have performed more quickly and easily themselves. We were included, and at our own pace. One of my jobs was to drain and crack the coconuts for ambrosia, our traditional Christmas dessert which was served with the doctored fruit cake, the amalgamation, and the burnt caramel. Auntie made it. Of course. Her good eye would flash while the glass one, impersonal and indifferent in its loose-lidded brimming lair, looked somewhere over my shoulder.

"I make the best ambrosia of anyone in this house, if I do say so myself."

She would let Jimmie Kate help her peel a half-bushel of oranges, but I was the one who tended to the coconut. I was the boy. Each coconut was a hard little rounded skull, maybe a shrunken head like that one in the museum at the State Capitol, covered with coarse, unkempt, shaggy hair that almost obscured the tiny slick black face at one end. It was a face. There were two rounded sightless eyes over a protruding O for a pouting mouth. It had to be a face; mummified and smoothed, half simian, faintly fetal, but what else but a face? Soon I would quit daydreaming and drive a nail deep through each eye and then the mouth and invert the whole over a glass. Mr. Jim liked to drink the juice.

"Save the coconut milk for Pa."

When the thin opalescent liquid stopped gurgling and dripping and I could no longer hear any sloshing when I shook the nut, I placed it on the well curbing and carefully tapped it with a hammer until it cracked into several pieces. Gingerly I pried the chunks of thick satin meat with adhering brown skin away from the shell and carried the pan full of fragrant coconut into the kitchen for Auntie to peel, wipe with a damp cloth, and grate. Christmas was dependent on Baby Jesus and Santa Claus, but this particular establishment needed me, also.

"Your mother is a fine woman, but she tends to get just a little too much sugar in her ambrosia."

Add the pungent oil of orange rind to the perfume of Christmas. One smelled it most when emptying the pan of bright twisting curls left by Auntie and Jimmie Kate, but it was also fragrant after supper to crease a piece of orange peel before a candle flame and watch the multicolored sputter and spark as the zest ignited. Those bursts were miniscule but were reminiscent, in the imaginative vision of a bemused child, of the magnificent display of sky rockets and Roman candles which were sure to be in our stockings on Christmas morning. If we had been good. And if Santa remembered that we had.

"I declare, boy, don't you know that playing in fire will make you wet the bed?"

Oh, sweet Baby Jesus, please don't let me pee on Pete.

Nothing contributed to the season like our father. He roared over the horizon like a comet; we were the dancers of the Aurora Borealis, flashing and leaping in his train. Forget all our cares, drop travail, ignore poverty. Eat, drink, and be merry, it's Christmas time. Whatever you do, be merry.

He was christened Ferrol Sams but he had more nicknames than anyone else I ever knew. Mother and LaLou called him "Pin"; Comp called him "Skipper"; Eugene called him "Brother." The hands called him variously "Cap'n," "Bossman," "Mista Fell." Simon, unwitting heir of who knows what relics of ancient and mysterious tongues, had a thicker, richer accent than anyone else on the farm. He referred to him as "Missa Pharaoh Sam," an appellation that did not seem incongruous to my ear. Simon may have had a weakness for alcohol and a grandiosity when imbibing it that made him the butt of jokes among his peers, but he was also perceptive and ingenious. It was he who inadvertently bestowed another nickname on my father. On a wintry Saturday afternoon, huddled with shortened necks against the blowing gray mist, a group of black men was gathered around the gas pumps of our uncle's store at Woolsey. One of Simon's braggadocian monologues was interrupted by a relatively sober and consequently impatient friend.

"Simon, hush yo mouf. You ain't got a dollar in yo pocket. I bet you ain't got a haffa dollar. You talk mighty big but I bet you ain't got a dime to yo name. Come on! Show us! Put up or shut up!"

Simon refocused his eyes. Ever affable, he grinned broadly and triumphantly proclaimed, "Who need cash money? Not none of me. I'n walk in at sto and git anything I want nout no money in my pocket. Cause I stays wid ne bare-headed man."

His attacker laughed. "Mista Fell got no use for a drunk nigger slobbering all over Woolsey on a Saridy afternoon."

"Yeah, he do too. He count on me lak I he right hand. He don't never wear no hat, and don't you put you mouf on him. I tell you I got ne world licked cause I stays wid ne bare-headed man. I stays wi' Missa Pharaoh Sam and he a real bear cat." The name stuck.

A generation later I lived to hear his grandchildren and great-grandchildren refer to him as "Bear Cat." And that to his face. The cousins called him Big Daddy. His own children evolved through changing address as the need arose to reinterpret periodically the charisma of this man. Bossman. Cap'n. Mista Fell. Missa Pharaoh. Bare-headed man. Bear Cat. Eventually, we used them all. Appropriately. At the time of which I write we called him Daddy. It was enough. We needed no more. It was a privilege.

Now came Christmas Eve, absolute and almost unbearable peak of anticipation. Would Santa Claus come?

"He's never missed so far but you never can tell."

Will he bring me anything?

"I'll just bet he will."

Have I been good enough?

"We'll just have to wait and see."

What time do you think he'll come?

"He won't come until every child in this house is asleep, and if he catches one peeking he'll spit tobacco juice in his eyes."

We believed.

Not a single menu for supper on Christmas Eve stands out in my memory. I remember everyone gathering in the parlor before the tree, from Mr. Jim and Miss Sis on down to the smallest child, while we listened to the first sixteen verses of the second chapter of Luke. Then we sang, our mother valiantly trying to keep us on pitch. "All is calm, all is bright." There was a temporary moment of peace, of total tranquillity. "Round yon virgin, mother and child."

We believed.

Then frenetic activity erupted again. We hung no stockings by the chimney with care; there was not room across the mantel piece for all of ours and our cousins'. Besides, there was a fire in the grate and they might burn. We draped them instead across the seats and over the knobs of chairs, along the sofa, on the end tables, anywhere. They were not special red or green Christmas stockings. They were our everyday, above-the-knee long stockings that we wore to school. They were clean, but they were likely to be old ones that were almost worn out; no need to subject good garments to the fraying stress of Santa Claus. We carefully pinned name tags made from tablet paper to our stockings. Jesus may have had the hairs on our heads numbered, but Santa Claus also did everything on an individual and personal basis.

Oh, how we believed.

Now we reverently set out a snack for Santa, a glass of buttermilk and the first piece of Auntie's fruit cake. One year Margaret Nelson, who had observed Pa Jim's pre-prandial hygiene, suggested that if Santa chewed tobacco we should also leave him a glass of water and a bucket so he could discard his cud and rinse his mouth. Auntie assured us that Santa could manage.

"Get along to bed now and go to sleep so he can come."

"Be sure to use the slop jar."

"Be sure to say your prayers."

"Quit that whispering and giggling."

"If you and Pete don't stop fighting we're going to separate you and make you sleep with the girls."

One year Miss Sis quieted the tumult from the foot of the stairs. I knew her for thirty years and in that time she never set foot on the second floor of that house where she was born except to comfort Aunt Pelly when Cousin Rebecca died. There was no need. She was like Jesus and could direct her minions from afar. She called up the stair well, "You children, hush. Listen. I think I hear Santa Claus."

Into the pulsating silence came the unmistakable sound of bell ringing, muted by distance but real as the cold air seeping under the baseboards and across the floor. Amid our excited gasps she admonished, "I thought I heard him cross directly over the house but y'all were making so much fuss I guess you scared him off."

Ellen Jane started crying. Audibly. Miss Sis relented. "Maybe he's just gone on down the road to the Stubbses'. Get real quiet now and I suspect he'll double back." Immediately ". . . all through the house not a creature was stirring, not even a mouse." That was one of the years when Pete still had faith. His instantaneous snores may have been affected but they were soporific. We slept. A quarter-century later, at our grandfather's funeral, Little Daddy, who was our father's youngest brother and the father of three of the cousins, laughed about gripping our dinner bell by its clapper while he slipped through the darkness all the way to the cow lot and rang it from the barn loft. In collusion with Miss Sis. I can still hear those faint notes ringing through the cold crisp darkness and they still do not sound at all like our dinner bell, but now

I believe Little Daddy. Everyone was important at Christmas.

Christmas morning did not begin at daybreak but at least two hours before. It began with the thump and patter of the newly wakened feet of children across the bare wood floors of a hundred-year-old farmhouse. No adult can sleep through that, no matter how accustomed to the regular night noises, the groans and creaks and sighs of such a house. At first we talked in whispers.

"Did he come?"

"I think I heard him but I went back to sleep."

"When can we go downstairs?"

"Maybe we'd better wait till we're sure he came."

"You better go pee; you're still dry."

Finally a permissive mother would light a lamp, and all Christmas would break loose. When some bolder child approached his bed to see if he was awake, Missa Pharaoh would leap up and startle the scout into immediate paralysis. "Christmas gift!" he would shout.

Then it rang all over the house.

"Christmas gift!"

You said it first and you said it fast. You said it to anyone and everyone upon first sight that day. It was the salutation of the season, used only on that particular morning. It was an achievement to catch a sister, a cousin, an aunt or uncle unawares with the cry.

"Christmas gift!"

They said we picked up the custom generations before from our darkies. Maybe so. Certainly their descendents all used it. It was said that whoever beat another person to saying it was supposed to receive a present from that individual. Whenever I said it to Simon or Coot or Clarence or any of Jesse Lee's children, however, I was always answered with, "Hand it here." My sister Janice had a sharp ear and had early noted the disregard for terminal consonant or sibilant in the speech of the help. She consequently cut a fraction of a second from her time. "Chrimma giff!" she would yell, jumping from behind a door. It was hard to get Christmas gift on Sister Janice.

It was impossible on Daddy. He beat everyone to it, his parents, his siblings, and certainly his children. He surprised, he startled, he anticipated everyone. It was a point of honor with him. He carried the custom into his eighties. He was even known to hide behind the smoke house and leap out at arriving grandchildren.

"Christmas gift!"

It is the cry of the Bear Cat. Of the Bareheaded Man. It brings Baby Jesus and Santa Claus together. It wraps them in red tissue paper adorned with a sprig of mistletoe or holly; it is a harmonious package.

It really means "I love you," and on that one morning each year it can be shouted exultantly to the heavens.

"Christmas gift!"

"Christmas gift! Everybody!"

In the darkness before dawn when the air of the world is thin and fresh, we assembled in the hall. So much energy crackled through and around us that nobody would have been surprised to see it sparking. Pa Jim ritualistically opened the door the merest crack, slipped into the parlor, and kindled a fire. He returned to stand before the closed door.

"He did come."

Amid urgent directions from adults and conflicting imprecations from our peers, we lined up. We did it by age. One year the oldest went first; the next year the youngest. When he was three and five, Little Eugene headed the line, and I'm not sure which year he was the proudest. By the time he was seven and nine he had become a bit blase and pretended modesty. Being a middle child meant I was never first, but it also meant I was never last. Either way I was always between Ellen Jane and Pete and was not big enough to see over either of them. As we waited for admission to the parlor on Christmas morning, no one jostled or shoved or fussed. It was probably our noblest moment.

When Miss Sis appeared and Pa Jim opened the door for her to march in, the gaggle of grandchildren swarmed close on her heels and fanned out to their individual stockings, the transformation of which was a delight. The flaccid brown stockings of the evening before were now magically stretched and stuffed to their limit, lumpy with manifold treasures, witness to the largess and magnanimity of Santa. Those bulging Christmas stockings were also subliminal witness to me that there was a flaw in the system. I had never been good enough over a whole year to merit equal reward with my virtuous sisters. Either the elves were not so omnipresent and omniscient as reported or else they had been remiss in their reports to the North Pole. The delicious feeling that guilt had not been assigned nor punishment impartially meted added to the special tingle of Christmas morning. Reprieve is sweet. If justice was going to roll down like a river, it at least was not forthcoming from Santa Claus but must await the

Baby Jesus, and anybody with peacock brains knew that was a long time away.

The contents of the stockings were traditional, fluctuating a trifle here or there with the degree of prosperity that year. The most eye-catching item was always the sky rocket. Each child received one of them and two Roman candles, along with firecrackers of varying sizes and a box of sparklers. The sky rocket protruded from the stocking gloriously, looking like a miniature of the water tank in Fayetteville, except that it had only one leg instead of four and was bedecked with red, white and blue bunting and sprinkled with five-pointed stars. The sky rocket was a responsibility. It was dangerous.

"Don't you get that thing too close to the fireplace, boy."

There was an apple in the stocking, an orange. Most years there was a tangerine, its watered-down flavor more than atoned for by the independent ease with which a child could peel it. There were bunches of raisins, still on branching golden twigs and still full of seeds. They were so plump and sweet that they gummed up everything if an exploring child squeezed them too hard when trying to guess the contents of a stocking before emptying it. There were hard candies scattered throughout, as brilliantly colored and painted as miniature tree ornaments, some of them with soft jelly centers and unfamiliar flavor. There was an assortment of nuts. The filberts were shaped like exotic acorns but sported brighter brown, nearly orange, shells. The few pecans were strangely striped and almost round, not products of any of our trees because I was personally familiar with the distinctive fruit from each individual tree in the family grove. This was another proof of the reality of Santa. No one in our thrifty family would have stooped to paying out good money for any product that was raised on the farm.

The English walnuts were as whorled and patterned as the golden brain of some tiny animal. They had fragile shells and waxed paper partitions and with careful cracking the meats could be extracted whole. The most treasured nut was the nigger-toe. Years later in the midst of prosperity and social progress, Carrie Colclough and I were reminiscing about the good old days.

"How come you white folks had to go and mess with nigger-toes? Seem like they just don't taste as good since they got changed over to Brazil nuts."

What a thrill they were. It was a skilled child who had learned with precisely what degree of force to wield a tapping rock so that the granular wooden shell would split and the polished boat-shaped kernel would not be smushed but could be extracted in thick and triumphant wholeness. A nigger-toe was a challenge.

Beside the stockings lay the individual gifts from Santa Claus for each child. The new jackets, the dresses, one year a pair of corduroy knickers for me, were dutifully exclaimed over and accepted, but it was the extra, the luxury item, that produced true joy. I watched Jimmie Kate one year as she politely feigned pleasure that Santa Claus had brought her a piano bench. I felt in my heart that she had never approached playing the piano for any purpose except to please the grownups. Her scales were plodding sounds from the imprisoning parlor, redolent of filial duty but totally lacking in spontaneity. Decades later, with the non-defensive pleasure of recalling childish peccadilloes, she confirmed this.

All of my sisters took. It was a badge of caste and culture. A scattering of refined and corseted ladies in the communities across the county opened their parlors to a privileged few and taught. The children of privilege took. Only an outsider would have stumbled at supplying the object of that verb. Since boys did not take, except for Griff, Jr., Ambrose, and Glendon, I was almost a grandfather before I fully appreciated the rigors of that discipline. In the same conversation when Jimmie Kate acknowledged her musical lassitude, Sara volunteered that she had actually hated piano lessons. The reason was that she took from Mrs. Perry and Mrs. Perry was mean. I remembered Mrs. Perry as a charming friend of our mother's, one who may have talked and walked a little rapidly and one who embodied bustling efficiency in the Baptist Church, but a lady who radiated affection and good will and was universally loved. For a while she wore little pinch-nose glasses that she pulled out on a chain from a button on her dress, and that was a most impressive thing to watch.

"Sara," I said in astonishment, "I can't believe Mrs. Perry had a mean bone in her body. What did she do?"

"She fussed and scolded if you hadn't practiced. And she kept an ice tea spoon in her lap and rapped your knuckles if you missed the same note twice. It used to make me want to cry, but of course you couldn't. You were too big for that."

I digested this revelation and then turned to Janice, the one considered tender-hearted, the one who had been frail in her youth, and also the one who had progressed farther in music. "Was Mrs. Perry mean to you?"

She thought a moment. "Not but once."

49

"Why?"

"Because the first time she fussed at me I wee-weed on her rug."

Janice reflected a moment. "It was awful. I had to go back to school wet, and my shoes and socks were squishy until time to go home. But Mrs. Perry was always real sweet to me."

The year that Santa Claus brought Jimmie Kate the piano bench, I saw our mother watch her as long as she could stand it and then she said, "Raise the lid, Jimps."

Within that hiding place for sheet music was stretched an entire collection of Little Colonel books. There was no feigning the happiness on my older sister's face as she let out a shriek and hugged everyone within reach. Christmas gift!

Also I watched my youngest sister on the morning when she discovered that she had indeed received a doll but not the particular one she had requested. Even in the years when we believed explicitly everything we were told, we still realized that the surest route to Santa's ear was via our parents and that prudent dissembling was mandatory. I recognized the struggle between her present disappointment and the hope of future reward, between desire and reality, between pragmatism and idealism. All this I saw on Sara's six-year-old face. I did not have the vocabulary to verbalize it but I had the perception to feel it as she took a long step from being a child toward becoming a lady. With only the faintest quiver of her lovely lower lip, like a thrush whose nest has been violated by a cow bird, she clasped the fledgling to her breast and buried her little freckled face in its hair. Christmas gift!

I remember the year of '29, foundation for the mindset of an entire generation about material security. The year was lean and mean. There was no extra gift of clothing or toys under my stocking in '29 and only one Roman candle kept the sky rocket company. With a shrug of acceptance I sat down and forced a leisurely exploration of the stocking. If that was all there was to North Pole joy that morning, it behooved me to prolong it. I examined each piece of candy, speculating on which colored designs went all the way through and which would come off with the first two sucks. I sorted the nuts into neat little piles. I set the firecrackers aside. When I extracted the raisins I pulled two off and ate them, ignoring the clinging lint from the stocking and being careful of the seeds. I knew that if you swallowed a watermelon seed it would sprout and grow inside you. My grandfather had told me that was what had happened to Cuddin John

McLean, and although it was absorbing to watch Cuddin John's watch fob jiggle in space while he led the singing on Sunday mornings, I had no desire to wake up some day with clusters of raisins hanging from my nose. There were perils in childhood greater than stepping on cracks.

At the very toe of my stocking was a foreign and unexpected object. On feeling it I imagined a dried biscuit. On delivery to vision it was a watch. A big, fat pocket watch. Like Pa Jim's, Comp's, Uncle Ed's. Like Daddy's. Mine was a shiny silver color, not white or yellow gold, but mine was thicker than any of theirs. Mine had Westclox on the face instead of Waltham or Hamilton, but mine ticked the loudest. Any forlornness vanished in an instant. I was a boy child. Some day I would be a man. Oh, Christmas gift!

Another Christmas morning of which I remember some vivid details was in a more affluent year. It was one of the times that LaLou brought with her from the opulence of Atlanta a gallon of fresh oysters for Auntie to put in the turkey dressing.

"A whole gallon? The menfolks can have some of them to eat with pepper sauce and we'll save some out for a stew. You shouldn't have spent that much, Addie Lou, but we can use them. They sure make the dressing richer. I don't mean to sound like I'm bragging, but the boarders at Woolsey always said my oyster dressing was the best they ever put in their mouths."

That was the Christmas that Santa Claus brought Ellen Jane and me bicycles, and that was the Christmas she and I quit believing in him. We were forced into it.

The protocol of belief was fairly well-defined. For several years a child had conviction. Then came the doubts. Often they were planted by an older child, often a schoolmate, one whose assumptions could be disregarded because for some reason he was usually not doing well in spelling or geography and lived in the academic danger of social promotion. The only thing he was good in was arithmetic. What did he know?

This was about the time that specific questions to parents about the mysteries and abilities of Saint Nicholas underwent a drastic reduction in number. No child was obtuse enough to probe so deeply into the matter that all his doubts about the reality of Santa Claus lay bare before mother or father. When knowledge about Santa Claus became too definite to deny, we stood naked in truth. The custom was to gather then around our persons the magic protection of the Emperor's Clothes so that we might remain believers, at least in our parents' eyes. The illusion of innocence was preferable to no innocence at all. Through ages four, five, and six our parents were able to fool us. Through ages eight, nine and even ten, we were able in turn to fool them. I think. Christmas gift!

Of all the cousins, Ellen Jane and I were probably the closest. Certainly we were in age. I played with her and competed with her, but I never pushed too far. She was two weeks younger than I but a good head taller. When goaded too far, she could thrash me. I adored her; affection so often germinates from respect.

She and I shared more than Christmas. In our infancy, home deliveries and breast feedings were the highest and best standards of medical care. No child got a bottle unless he was weasly or had a mother who was delicate. Mothers stayed home out of necessity to be there when babies became hungry, for they were equipped with what my elders called "the dinner jug." The act of nursing was a modest act, one conducted in privacy, certainly out of sight of any menfolk, sometimes beneath a sheltering scarf or napkin. Aunt Ara was Ellen Jane's mama. She was the one who introduced brown eyes into our gene pool and her children consequently differed from the rest of us in appearance.

When Ellen Jane and I were babies, Little Daddy and Aunt Ara lived right across the field from us. That was when he still thought he could make a living farming and before he went to work for a road contractor. Our mothers, I was told in lowered voice, both had lots of milk. Certainly both ladies were full of energy and loved to be on the go. They were ideal baby-sitters for each other and their two babies were fed simultaneously, abundantly, and indiscriminately while the freed mother of the moment enjoyed carefree shopping or missionary meetings. The Common Cup. Mother's Day Out.

"You and Ellen Jane mustn't fuss with each other. In some ways she's closer than your sisters."

Auntie's elucidation was explicit but ladylike, although tinged with what I later identified as nulliparous wistfulness. Ambrosia, amalgamation cake and oyster dressing were a matter of perspective. When I became enough of an adult to realize that accomplishments are relative, I loved Auntie unconditionally. At the time I was outraged. My mother would never have shared my pottage which was also my birthright with another child, and that one a girl to boot.

Maybe Auntie was making it up to tease me. I consulted the Oracle of Delphi down at the woodpile. Mr. Jim cut a chew of tobacco so thin that it curled on itself and popped it into his mouth. "Sure, boy, that's the way it was. Y'all were what we call 'titty twins.' It was convenience, not necessity like some folks. Use to in old days, if a mama's milk was thin and the baby weasly, we'd get a colored woman who had lately freshened, one we knew was clean, to help out. Nothing unusual about that. Have to do it with calves now and then to this day, but you have to hold the cow. She'll kick and butt."

I was repelled. As an innocent, unsuspecting baby I had been periodically deserted to feed from an alien breast, to pull at a foreign pap, to fend off starvation the best I could with brown-eyed milk. Worse than that, my inherited bounty had been casually shared with another. Ellen Jane was probably bigger than I was because by some quirk of fate she had always managed to get the richer breast, wherever she happened to be suckling. I accosted my mother with diffidence and a little distrust. She assured me that this had been a happy time, a wonderful arrangement, that it was like having real twins, that there had been plenty to go around. The bond that I forged with Ellen Jane, nevertheless, was always tinged with just the faintest guilt of a secret that, if it was no longer dark, in my judgment should have been. I ate my peas, I gorged on cornbread, but I never caught her in growth. She had too good a head start.

The Christmas that I remember my titty twin most poignantly was the year we were confronted with harsh reality about Santa Claus, that year of the bicycles. Hers was blue and mine was red, and they glistened in the parlor beside our stockings with as much reflecting shine as the ornaments on the tree, so spanking new I felt they would squeak if I touched them. After daylight came and we were out in the yard trying to master them, we fell to assuring each other that Santa Claus did not have to do things exactly the way our ordinary perceptions dictated. My postulate was that a being who was capable of getting down a two-story chimney that had a coal-burning grate at the bottom of it surely had sense enough to unhook the front door and roll a couple of bicycles in, especially if he had just eaten that terrible tasting fruitcake and was full of buttermilk. Ellen Jane mused that perhaps he had brought them unassembled down the chimney in his pack and then put them together in the parlor while we slept. "In a twinkling," she said.

Pete overheard us. He was a year and a half older and at least a decade wiser. He lived in Atlanta.

"You two ninnies quit making up fairy tales and come with me."

He led us behind the barn where he had been potting at Mr. Jim's pigeons with his new air rifle and pointed. Secreted inside a shed, awaiting disposal, stood two card-board cartons from Sears Roebuck, a picture of a girl's bike on one, of a boy's bike on the other. The papers diagramming their assembly were crumpled and stuffed loosely in the cartons.

"There! Now I guess you'll believe me. I've been know-ing for three years but my mama said she'd snatch me bald-headed if I told you two. Besides, my daddy said driving down here he knew he'd be late getting to bed because he'd have to help Comp put y'all's bikes together. Said neither one of your daddies would get it right."

That statement about the daddies smacked of truth even more irrefutably than the empty cartons.

Ellen Jane burst into tears and fled toward the house. I followed her, ineffectual but loyal. We encountered Aun-tie on the back doorsteps.

"Girl, what are you crying about this time? You've got to quit being so tender-hearted. I declare you traipse around here sometimes like your bladder was behind your eyeballs."

We veered abruptly at a right angle and leaned in the sheltering corner of the east chimney. Ellen Jane hushed.

I borrowed from the wisdom of my grandfather in his assessment of one of our neighbors. "Don't pay any attention to Pete. He'd climb a tree to tell a lie when he could stand on the ground and tell the truth." Ellen Jane hiccupped, but her soft shining eyes were non-acquiescent.

"Besides," I added staunchly, clinging to the myth for her benefit, "who's to say Sears Roebuck doesn't have a branch store at the North Pole?"

Ellen Jane burst into tears again and I lapsed into silence. Truth is truly naked when it appears explosively, and it can be painful when one is not even afforded the temporary dignity of the Emperor's Clothes.

As soon as the stockings had been explored and the gifts of Santa assessed, we had the tree. The individual presents from child to child, from child to parent, to grandparent, to aunt, to uncle, to cousin were removed from beneath the tree and from among its branches and distributed. It was not until well after the advent of Roosevelt that there were gifts on our tree from adult to adult. Compromise with economics was expedient, necessary.

"We all know we love each other; Christmas is for children."

Wrappings were removed and exaggerated exclamations of surprise and appreciation forthcoming. We were all thoroughly indoctrinated with the philosophy that it's the thought, not the gift, that counts. Thanks for the celluloid pencil sharpener. Christmas gift!

By the time the presents were all removed, daylight was showing gray through the windows and the tree stood thick and dark, deflowered. Somehow its tinsel, its balls, its icicles, never seemed quite so bright after dawn on Christmas morning. We had to eat breakfast before we could go outside to play with our treasures or shoot firecrackers, and we were herded into the dining room. Auntie always slipped out early from the parlor so that we could have fresh biscuits; my grandparents would have vaporized instantaneously into ghosts if they had ever been confronted with toast at breakfast. We also had fresh sausage. Some was spicy hot, festive with the crim-

son flakes and flat little seeds of red pepper, but a separate batch without pepper had been made for the children and Miss Sis.

"I declare, I do believe I got just a little too much sage
in it this year. Or maybe it tastes that way because I don't
have quite enough salt."

The sausage was perfect; the chorus of reassurance
overwhelming. Always. Miss Sis would sip her Postum
and Mr. Jim would saucer and slurp his coffee and even
they would take the trouble to tell Sack the sausage was
just right.

We also had brains-and-eggs. They were prepared at
the last minute by our mother, who stood over a sauce
pan, poached the hog brains without ever letting them
boil, and then scrambled them with soft eggs. Auntie did
not do brains. Whatever kudos accrued from them was
not begrudged. It was not all that bad a dish when stirred
with grits and chewed with a bite of the adult sausage,
but most of the children stood with Auntie. There were
always plenty of brains to go around.

There were plenty of biscuits, too. Auntie saw to that.
If there were no biscuits left over she would berate herself
for not having cooked enough. She made them from
whole wheat flour which we called "graham" and she

made them from scratch, starting with a sour, yeasty wad left from the previous day's breakfast. She added salt, baking powder, lard, soda, and buttermilk in quantity and proportion known only to her and never duplicated since. She pinched off individual portions of the dough, rolled them expertly between her palms, smeared them on each side with swift pass through grease in a preheated pan, and popped them into the oven of the wood-burning stove. Those biscuits were buttered so hot that Auntie had to keep flipping them in her hands.

"I believe to my soul I got just a pinch too much soda in them this morning. Those drummers at Woolsey always loved my biscuits."

They were perfect recipients for syrup, of which there were two kinds. We had ribbon cane for Mr. Jim and most of the rest of us, and we also had sorghum for Comp, who called himself a ridgerunner because he was from Tennessee. He liked his syrup green-tinted and acrid and so thick you could cut it with a knife. Mr. Jim always made the ribbon cane syrup himself and cooked it so thin that it ran all over the plate.

"A youngun can't ever hem my syrup up with just one biscuit."

Aunt Ara was from north Georgia and laughingly called herself a hillbilly when Comp said he was a ridgerunner and then would say, "Please pass the sorghum." I did not see how she could really like it the best. She was just being nice to Comp, I thought, because they were both in-laws and she figured he needed company. We ran out of ribbon cane with its glints of red and gold every year, but there was never a dearth of sorghum. I occasionally wondered what that thick sharp syrup might have done to breast milk, but I never broached the question.

After breakfast, we were bundled up and allowed outdoors to play while the women began fixing Christmas dinner. Indeed, we were herded out and were encouraged to remain outside.

"That door's got a bad breath; quit banging in and out. If you children don't stay out of my kitchen, I declare somebody's going to get scalded."

Christmas Day was supposed to be cold. Most years it was. Our favorite play consisted of shooting our fire-crackers. There were packs of one hundred small ones with their fuses woven together to hold them in two neat rows. They were wrapped in flimsy, gaily colored paper that showed, beneath rows of Chinese calligraphy, yellow-skinned children in their bathrobes sporting pigtails and obviously having a good time. Their eyes were so slanted and their smiles so wide that we fancied their pigtails had been plaited too tightly, but they were assurance that our Lottie Moon pennies must have been used effectively.

Pa Jim would bring a shovel of hot coals from the fireplace and set it down away from leaves or trash or outbuildings that might catch afire, cautioning us to be careful. He never mentioned bed-wetting. Grandfathers were lofty creatures and there were some things that were beneath their notice. That shovel full of coals was a treasure. Incandescent when first borne forth, the embers outdoors soon looked dead. They became covered with fine white ash until a resurrecting wind or a puffing child blew on them to exhibit once again the glowing red. Touching the tip of a firecracker to a live coal produced a fizz and sputter that impelled one to hurl the firecracker away as fast as possible. Add a whiff of gunpowder to the perfume of Christmas.

It was a cool daredevil of a child who could hold a sizzling firecracker long enough to take aim. I always cast

mine away in haste, trading off the satisfaction of personal safety against the glee of causing cousins or sisters to jump away from an imminent explosion beneath their feet. I had been exposed to Biscuit Hand at school in Fayetteville. He was older than I and greatly admired because he was tough. He kept blowing his fingers off and had the aura on the school ground of a wounded veteran, a hero who nevertheless walked modestly before his fellows. To be sure, it was with dynamite caps and not firecrackers that Biscuit mutilated himself, restlessly searching, I suppose, for a bigger and better bang. I had no wish to emulate him; a firecracker never exploded anywhere near my hand.

A safer, more controlled entertainment with firecrackers was to shoot them off under a tin can. It muted the noise of explosion but it was a satisfaction to watch the cans sail high into the air, usually straight up but occasionally tumbling end over end. Very rarely, by twisting fuses together, we could effect firing in stages, and it was a thrill to watch a can jerk and change course in midair when a tardy firecracker blew up inside it. Of course for this pastime, we needed another ignition system than the pan of embers. Matches were available but were expensive and also not dependable if a breeze blew

up. We solved the dilemma by wheedling a lighted cigarette from one of the menfolks. Blow on the end of a
cigarette and it would last down to your fingertips. Pete
would look over his shoulder and take a forbidden puff
when the fire was needed. Sometimes he had three-inch
or even five-inch firecrackers that Santa had not brought
but that he had procured for himself in Atlanta. The
three-inch ones would sail a tin can all the way over the
holly tree, and the five-inch ones would blow a can to
smithereens about ten inches off the ground and excavate
the launching site. In my eyes Pete was as daring, as
casually heroic, as Biscuit Hand. It was a good thing we
had no dynamite caps.

A couple of hours after sunup, the hands began drifting
in. If we looked up from our play we could see
them on the big road. I do not remember ever seeing one
alone; they came by twos or threes; they approached at a
contented stroll, leisurely, almost dream-like. No work to
do on that day, no mules to harness, no hogs to kill. They
would not stay to dinner nor would they be invited. Most
of them would hang around in the yard and not even

come inside. They came to the Big House with purpose, however. They dressed in new overalls and jumpers that had not yet accommodated to body creases and were stiffer than the protocol under which we lived. They came as neighbors, not tenants, certainly not servants. There were courtesy and affection in their bearing. They came to the Big House as friends. On Christmas Day in the morning.

Across the years I remember them. Willie Floyd, Jesse Lee, and Simon, who had married the sisters, Parthinia, Matt, and Odessa. Alf Gooden; Paul Arnold. Fred, Jesse, and Willie Porter, who bore the same surname as my grandmother for the very good reason that they were the sons of Uncle Andrew, who had been willed to her when she was six. There were Coot and Clarence, jocular noisy brothers who shared the same house. Clarence couldn't stay married but always wanted to; Coot didn't particularly care if he was married or not and his wife was a limpet, cooking and cleaning for both of them without complaint. Paul Kennel, dapper with his hair-line mustache, usually walked down with George and Wes, who were sons of Uncle John and Aunt Lou. Uncle John was a true patriarch. In the last really good cotton year he cleared a tremendous amount of cash and led his family in hegira to Detroit in a white Buick touring car. After 1929 they all came back to the farm, but by then Uncle John was feeble. He didn't work in the fields and he didn't walk the big road on Christmas Day. There was Lisbon, who had married Uncle John's oldest daughter, Lucinda, and had the air of being as sturdy inside as he was outside. There was Central Harp who died one Saturday night because a well-meaning town marshall did not know that he shouldn't jerk out the switchblade that was embedded to its hilt through his skull. There was Bud Hunt with his son, Hubert. Bud had married again and had four stepsons who were good plow hands but he treated them as children and left them at home.

I remember them all. My father shouted, "Christmas gift!" at them and they shouted back. Then they invariably said, "Hand it here!" and he did. Amidst laughter and loud voices he handed out packages my mother had wrapped, socks or scarves in the lean years, flannel shirts in the fat ones. Lean or fat, hot or cold, hell or high water, he also handed over a crisp new bill. Rarely a twenty, sometimes a ten, never less than a five, and to hell with Hoover. They were always new bills, crisp and never creased, and they snapped as he pulled them from their packet. The bare-headed man had his pride.

He also had a jug. The girls were shooed around the house to play, their delicate sensibilities not to be violated by the ensuing ritual. I was a boy. I could watch. We were behind the engine house or around the corner of the smokehouse, outside the vision of Miss Sis, imperious queen of the Court of Temperance. The surreptitious appeal of this moment was heightened by knowledge of her disapproval as well as of the law of the land. There were rights of man and rites of season that transcended Constitutional amendments. All hail the hamadryad. The jug was passed.

Bud Hunt was a deacon and did not drink, but even he touched his tongue in politeness to the mouth of the jug. Simon always swung it so high and held it so long that the next communicant had to wrest it from him.

"At's white man likker and hit sho good. Crimma giff! Wait'll ney see nis quenty dollar bill over at Woolsey. One nem on me just nother day and say you tote yo head like you think you ne king of England. Which you do, Missa Pharaoh Sam, you do tote yo head. You all time tote yo head. Me an you got ne world licked."

At the end of the line my father stood. He upended the jug for a ceremonial pull himself and then proffered it on strongly hooked forefinger for second helpings before replacing the corn-cob stopper. Then he always said, "Merry Christmas to all of you!" The Common Cup. Father's day out. Christmas gift was over but it was still Christmas Day. About this time Little Daddy, and later Pete when he was older, was likely to toss a five-incher in the midst of the forest of feet, effecting dispersal that was jostling, hilarious and explosive.

A little before noon the other company came. First Haynia and Charles. We called her Sister. She was the oldest child, the first daughter of our grandparents, the unimpeachability of such rank commanding a respect and deference that might not otherwise have been forthcoming. No breath of criticism was ever voiced in front of the children, for "Respect your elders" was high in the family Decalogue, about three rules up from "Don't discuss personal business in front of the help." These dicta probably served to sharpen our skills of observation, and the children were never fooled much longer than the hands. There was the feeling that no one in the family thought Sister had married well. It was years before this was confirmed by eavesdropping.

"I know he's never been a good provider but you mustn't say he's sorry as gully dirt; after all, he's in the family. Of course, you know and I know he never was a good catch in the first place and Haney wouldn't have married him if he hadn't been so handsome and had that new buggy. I'm glad I waited till I was an old maid. Pretty is as pretty does. I've done very well if I do say so myself."

Sister had a black coat with a whole black fox snugged around her neck for a collar. The eyes of that fox were glass but they glared with malevolence and its little white teeth were displayed in a snarl. She never said "Christmas gift!" herself and responded to our salutation with an aloof and tolerating smile. We soon quit saying it to her. This was in contrast to LaLou, who had a brown coat with a golden brown fox whose eyes twinkled, whose teeth smiled. LaLou was Pete's mama, had graduated from Bessie Tift, and taught school, but still she laughed a lot. She was the first in the family to manifest that real ladies could get a permanent wave and that short hair was not just the flag of the flapper.

"It takes a deal of getting used to, but I declare, Lou, I'll have to break down and say it's right becoming to you."

"Why, thank you, Sack. I'll tell you one thing; a bob is sure a sight easier to look after."

All of us knew LaLou loved us without her saying so, and she could holler "Christmas gift!" with the best of us.

Sister on Christmas morning sat in Mammy's room and visited with her. LaLou was always busy in the kitchen helping Mother and Auntie and Aunt Ara get dinner. Charles would speak to everyone, receive a distracted answer and then would wander out to the smokehouse or the engine room and cadge a drink. The hands would disperse more quickly at his advent than in response to a firecracker, but without any laughter.

Bubba Hugh and Aunt Pelly came from Barnesville and, with timing perfected through years of practice, arrived right at dinner time. Bubba Hugh was the oldest son. He ran a filling station and raised pecans for a living, but he stirred up trouble for recreation. He would bring up subjects in open family conversation that were supposed to be hush-hush, taboo, dead and buried. Then he would sit back and chortle until he was red in the face at the fire storms he created. He knew all about Auntie getting churched in her youth for dancing. He had brazenly worked against Daddy when he ran against Mr.

Culpepper for the legislature. He always told everybody as soon as he found out that Mammy had changed her will again. He was the uncle who rewarded me with his favor over all my siblings and cousins, and I, distinct from all of them, adored him.

"Now, Hugh, don't you go digging up any of those old bones. This is Christmas, for mercy sakes."

My Daddy and Comp and Ed Giles and Little Daddy wouldn't think of letting their wives drive if they were in the car, but Bubba Hugh always arrived with Aunt Pelly as his chauffeur. He was a sight. He carried a walking stick made of hickory with three inches of lead pipe affixed to the end of it. My daddy said, "Hugh Sams is the only man I've ever seen who could knock the living hell out of someone and never quit smiling." The pipe at the end of the walking stick added the ominous thrill of potential force to Bubba Hugh's charisma.

He wore his pants up under his armpits, supported there by stout suspenders, and he carried a nickel-plated .38, barrel end up, in his hip pocket. You could unfailingly pick out his hat from the hat rack, for he had worn it so long it looked like him. He wore it on the side of his head, rakish, jaunty, defiant. It was fun to watch him eat or to chew tobacco. He had had no teeth for at least thirty years before I knew him, and when his jaw went into motion his chin very nearly touched his nose. When I was older I asked about the teeth.

"You know your Uncle Hugh has spells. Pelly carried him to every doctor she could think of and nothing did any good. Finally, one in Griffin told her that his teeth were poisoning Brother's system and Pelly tricked him into the hospital for what she told him were tests. When Brother woke up he didn't have a tooth in his head and he told her, 'You got 'em out, Pelly, now by God let me see you get some back in.' And she never has. We don't talk about that, it's a sore subject with Pelly." We didn't talk about the spells, either. Bubba Hugh didn't start having them until he was kicked in the head by a horse after he was a grown young man and married. Over the years he had discovered for himself that a good strong drink of whiskey was a satisfactory preventative for most of his spells and even during Prohibition, and even in the hallowed presence of my grandmother, he traveled with a bottle. Aunt Pelly kept tight control of it, however, and sometimes he would actually have to shake and tremble for fascinating minutes before she would give him a drink.

Another thing we didn't talk about was that Aunt Pelly and Bubba Hugh were first cousins. We never got details of any family consternation their wedding may have caused, only a confidential lowering of the voice when kinship was being clarified. Auntie would get a tight line to her lips.

"We worried a little about the children, but they all three were beautiful and turned out well. Rack was high in his class at West Point. And everybody knows that Sara Jane is the best nurse who ever finished at Piedmont Hospital. Dr. Sauls and Dr. Boyd both told me so when Pa was up there with his gland."

There is nothing in a Southern family that can be as attractive to a child as a relative with characteristics that we don't talk about. Bubba Hugh was consequently replete with mystery and absolutely compelling of attention. I learned more thespian tricks and manipulative maneuvers from him than from anyone else in my experience. He had a marvelous sense of the ridiculous, an unerring eye but an accepting tolerance for human foibles, and he could tell stories that kept me spellbound. Any time his jaws were in motion, I paid attention. I learned a lot.

Once he extracted a pint bottle from his hip pocket behind the engine house and said to his brother-in-law, "Charlie, if you want a pull of this, make haste before one of the children shows up or Mammy catches us." I watched as Charlie Wilson turned the bottle heavenward and I saw his Adam's apple bob three times. Then I saw him spit and spray the holly tree that had been planted the day my grandmother was born as he yelled, "Good God, Hugh, what in the hell is that?" I watched the twinkle and the exaggerated look of innocence as Bubba Hugh moved his jaws as smooth as feather pillows.

"Now, Charlie, don't get excited. I rinsed the bucket out real good and set it on a flat rock behind my cow just this morning. That was a clean catch."

BuMawt and Aunt Linnie lived at Woolsey and they had Christmas at home with their grown and married children. He smoked Chesterfields in a cigarette holder almost as long as Roosevelt's, and you could pick his hat off the rack, too. He was high sheriff of Fayette County, ran a store, had a cotton gin, and farmed more acres than our daddy. He drove Buick automobiles, was rich as Croesus, and always gave a child a sucker at his store. He may not have laughed all the time, but in my memory he does. We loved BuMawt. Aunt Linnie was blue-eyed and beautiful and had enough of a tremor to make her voice quaver a little. She was one of the many daughters of Mr. Geedie Gay, who was reported to have said, "Aye, hoot! The devil owed me a debt and he paid me off in sons-in-law." Aunt Linnie and BuMawt came in the afternoon to see Miss Sis and Mr. Jim, but they never tarried long. BuMawt had more sense and protective diplomacy than to hang around a gathering very long that included Bubba Hugh and the enticing targets of all his brothers and sisters. It wasn't that BuMawt didn't like to fight; he just couldn't stand fussing. Especially when Bubba Hugh had stirred it up and then was standing off to the side laughing and chewing tobacco.

"Lou, do you and Mawt know that Mammy has changed her will again? You've all been disinherited, even Ferrol. Sack gets everything. It doesn't bother me because I sold my share of the estate to Ferrol twenty years ago, but I thought y'all might be interested."

"Hush your mouth, Hugh. Sack deserves anything she gets; you can stir up more commotion than a weasel in a henhouse, but you can't make me mad at Christmas."

We at the Big House packed into the dining room for Christmas dinner. That meal was the fruition of weeks of work, the supreme and extravagant celebration of an entire year. My mother couldn't get away with reading any more Scriptures that would point up the true meaning of Christmas, but she was careful about who she asked to say the blessing. Pa Jim and Daddy never responded with more than the one sentence supplication that was offered in a routine monotone at all our meals; Little Daddy was asked once and said loudly, "I beg to be excused"; Charles and Bubba Hugh were never invited. Mother wanted something special by way of a Christmas blessing, and in that era it had to be delivered by a man.

Ed Giles and Comp were the favored ones. Ed Giles was a great favorite in the family. He was a half-head shorter than LaLou but he laughed a lot and seemed to have developed a satisfactorily protective armor against the arrows of connubial bossiness. He was slickly bald in an upward slant from his eyebrows to the crown of his head, and the tufts on each side were so thick that I felt if they ever got away from the barber he would look like the secretary bird on the Arm and Hammer card. Looking at his head made one think that Ed Giles was standing on tiptoe. He could offer up a good prayer, and was given to calling first names when asking the Lord for blessings, never forgetting, however, to include the more impersonal poor-and-sick-wherever-they-may-be.

Comp spoke louder, albeit with more pauses for clearing his throat, and his blessings tended to outlast the average child's patience. He requested remembrance of the true meaning of this day and thanks for Thy Son and always concluded with a quite proper division of labor when he dedicated our lives to His service and this food to the nourishment of our bodies. When Comp prayed I was always so concerned with my desire for the latter that I was restive about the former. Comp was my mother's favorite supplicant, however, and I suspect that a tally would have shown him leading Ed Giles by a good three to one.

It was not that my mother liked Comp any better than she liked Ed Giles. I suspected that it was because she had been present when Comp accepted Christ as his personal Saviour, acknowledged it by public profession of faith at Woolsey Baptist Church, and was subsequently baptized in the cool and annealing, although somewhat murky, waters of Burch's Pond. Comp had been a World War I buddy of our father's and as far as my mother was concerned had turned his back on sin, and a little away from my father, when he married Auntie and waded fully clothed behind Reverend Widener into the dammed-up flow of Woolsey Creek that Sunday afternoon. He even wore a coat and tie, which was the most extreme dedication ever manifested by anyone in Burch's Pond. His World War I demons must have contrived to plague him at times, for I heard him pray most fervently once at revival meeting that the Lord would give him patience, a petition I neglected to take personally. Now I realize I should have. Many years later when Auntie developed Alzheimer's and would not let him out of her sight, I remembered that prayer.

When I was a child, however, I chafed for him to hush so that Christmas dinner could begin. I was always grateful that my father and grandfather assumed that food would go for the nourishment of my body and didn't waste time petitioning for it. I thought that Mr. Jim and the Bear Cat were Christians right enough, saved as anybody, but I also regarded them as Baptist-proof. When the time came they might have to trail behind their wives into the Promised Land, into that far-off sweet forever just beyond the shining river, into our Father's House of Many Mansions, but while they dwelled on this earth they strode as giants and, as such, they were exempt from certain minutiae.

After dinner, with the whole tribe gorged and sated, turkey bones shining white and drying on the platter, dishes washed, the horde of happy dogs replete with table scraps, we children were sent out to play again. With our rewards for the recent pressure of being astoundingly good now safely in hand, there was release from fear of retribution. Santa Claus was 365 days away; the elves were surely too tired to notice us; Jesus was still a little bitty baby. As only cousins and siblings can, we immediately fell to fussing. We were separated. Some of us were made to take naps. On Christmas Day in the afternoon.

The women visited in Mammy's room. The men played Rook in the dining room. At first the former group was the more interesting to me, but at about age eight I became bonded to the latter. My grandmother did not allow real cards in our house; they had pictures of devils, demons, witches, and Jezebels on them. Real cards were either symbols of Roman Catholic license or else they represented forces from the darker world, and the difference was too finitely nice to delineate. It was easier for her to flash her eyes in command than to make explanatory pronouncements. Real cards were banned.

Rook cards were permitted. There was no way people could gamble or otherwise sin while playing Rook. Its deck consisted of only numbered cards in four different colors. The sole picture in the deck was the Rook, which looked for all the world to me like a crow holding a fan in one claw. It not infrequently turned up in the widow and was rich reward for a bid.

Pa Jim and Ed Giles played partners, Comp and Skipper. Always. They had played together so long that they had honed the game to the pace of experts. The first four cards from each suit were dropped, the minimum opening bid was ninety. They were serious, aggressive, competitive. They indeed did not play for money; they played for blood. They played in a cloud of tobacco smoke fueled by Mr. Jim's pipe, Daddy's Lucky Strikes, Ed Giles's Chesterfields, and Comp's roll-your-own Targets, which he fashioned nightly on a little machine so that they looked as tailor made as anyone else's but were considerably cheaper. Except for review of the previous hand while the cards were being shuffled, they played in silence broken only by expletives, or exhortations to "trump that goddam fourteen." Comp and Ed Giles did not curse. They never took the Lord's name in vain, but neither did they fling caution to the wind and risk lightning bolts to walk like giants across the hand. The two teams were well-balanced. On Christmas Day in the afternoon.

Enveloped in the blue, eye-stinging, stifling haze produced by four enthusiastic tobacco addicts, I watched, and thought that these men were geniuses. They always seemed to know how many trumps were still out, where the much desired but dreaded Rookie was, and where the higher cards reposed. Then I started watching eyes. A wink when the cards were first picked up meant that the player had the Rookie, a wink when a card was placed in play meant that the player had the boss, a wink from an opposing player to his partner meant that he had a void and could trump that trick. My grandfather had the slickest wink of all, but my father was close behind. Better not mess with giants.

It was absolutely exciting to an eight-year-old. I had discovered a secret cave where treasure was surely hidden. Then I began watching the fingers. For bidding purposes the fingers had identity to match the colored cards. A wiggle of the forefinger meant black, middle finger red, ring finger green, and little finger yellow. Counting the rapid wiggles revealed the number of cards in each suit. By then I was nine years old. The Emperor's Clothing apparently was common garb around my house. The cave grew deeper, darker. After my grandfather died, I broached the subject to my father for the first time, wondering why they had bothered.

"Well now, son, that was stiff competition; we were just helping each other with a few little signals. Don't you ever let me hear you say we were cheating; that's a fighting word. All we were doing was having a little friendly game. Just in the family."

During the game, Bubba Hugh prowled the yard and the outbuildings with his walking stick, waiting for three-thirty when he could feel a spell coming on successfully enough to entice Aunt Pelly into producing his prophylactic elixir. Charles wandered The Place lonely as a cloud; he had learned years ago behind the engine house that he wanted no interchange with Bubba Hugh and apparently no one wanted any with him. To us he was neither fish, fowl, nor good red herring; interesting conversation would halt and change direction when he appeared. Pretty soon he would wander inside.

"Honey, get your things together; I reckon we better be going."

Sister's departures were events of such leisure it was difficult to distinguish them from tedium. They did not occur until accompanied, over ritualistic and superficial protestations, by enough food from the feast to last for several days. I remember that Sister liked white meat. I also remember that, although she regularly carried off a Mason jar of ambrosia, she was not once given any of the fruitcake. Eventually she would remind Charles to help her into the coat with the mean fox, she would remember at least three things she had neglected to tell Mammy, and then they would be gone.

When Aunt Pelly and Bubba Hugh bid their farewells, the Rook game broke up, at least for a few minutes, and there was more than a little hubbub, with Aunt Pelly promising everybody to come again soon. She had wavy, snow-white hair and a dainty little parrot nose that came from the Gay side of her family. Sams noses were typically aquiline, but our branch was diluted with Porter genes and tended to smear out over the face by the time hair turned white.

"Y'all come see us, too, you hear?"

Bubba Hugh climbed into the car holding his walking stick like the scepter of the kingdom and cast me one last roguish look before they left. The twinkle in his eye seemed to confide that he knew a lot more than I did, that most of it was funny, and that some day we would get together. When I was old enough. Bubba Hugh always made me feel chosen.

When the company was all gone, the Rook game all finished, Christmas Day in the afternoon was on the down slide. Only the true cadre of Christmas was left in the old house, Mammy and Pa, Millen and Pin, Sack and Comp, Lou and Ed, Ara and Gene. And us. The children. At dusk dark we gathered in the dining room once again and with diminished enthusiasm picked at our supper. Oyster dressing tasted better fresh.

After the dishes were washed, everybody gathered on the front porch while the menfolks helped us with the remaining fireworks from our stockings. The sparklers looked like wires that had been dipped in molten lava and allowed to harden. They took forever to ignite, but we were allowed to hold them by ourselves. The girls delighted in tracing glowing arabesques in the dark of the front porch. Pete was an expert at throwing a lighted sparkler so high in the air that it came bouncing down through the bare branches of the old oak and sometimes burned out before it hit the ground. There was not much else a boy child could do with a sparkler, but the girls loved them.

We all loved the soughing intake and hiccupping whoosh of a Roman candle and the slightly jarring belch as another colored ball erupted from the cardboard cylinder that we kept rotating so the fire would not go out. Finally it was stand back for the sky rockets. Of the children, only Pete was occasionally allowed to light one and even he would scamper to a safe distance when the fuse sputtered. Sky rockets were strictly a spectator activity, and despite the grandeur and glory of their mid-heaven explosions they were always a little saddening. They were the last fireworks to be ignited from our stockings of that morning. They would sigh and hiss in spiral loft through the heaven all the way above the trees and across the fields. They released in fiery orgasm a brilliant scattering of blue and red and green and yellow and even purple balls which fell over Jesse Lee's or Lisbon's or Simon's house and disappeared in fading fall on the drift of the same mysterious current that had assisted Santa the night before. A sky rocket was magic. It had been a long day, an exciting day, a totally fulfilling day, and underlying the awe, the marvel at the sky rockets, was the wistful knowledge that this was the end. This was Christmas Day in the evening and it was over.

We did not have to be shooed to bed on Christmas night. Life was back to normal. On the quick ritualistic good night trip to the grandparents' room I gave only a cursory look at Mammy's hearth to see if any fire babies were visible. Auntie had taught Jimmie Kate about fire babies and Jimmie Kate had taught me. I soon discounted their reality, but I think Jimmie Kate herself believed in fire babies long after she became knowledgeable about Santa Claus. After a quick hug and kiss from Mammy and Pa, we were only too glad to head upstairs, yearning for sleep. In contrast to Christmas Eve, there was peace on the pallets that night.

So. It was over. We grew up. World War II came and went. The grandparents died. Then the aunts and uncles. The sisters and I married. We all had children. We settled into homes in the county, the sisters on The

Place, almost within shouting distance of each other. Our own children were now the cousins. We stayed in our individual homes on Christmas Eve but we all descended on the Big House on Christmas Day. On Christmas Day in the morning.

The Bear Cat laughed exultantly and apprehended every arrival. "Christmas gift!" rang exultantly. Janice still said "Crimma giff!" and beat everyone but Daddy. Miss Mildred still had the tree in the parlor and we all lined up to go in, except the protocol alternated no more; it was always the youngest who got to open the door. We had Scripture, prayer, carols, and Santa Claus. In that order.

"Oh, we are blessed. Let's don't give each other gifts; it's enough just to be together and love one another. Let's remember the true meaning of Christmas. But if you are going to get me another dress this year, be sure it has long sleeves."

Then they died. Both of them. In the house. At home. First Missa Pharaoh; the next year to the exact month, as a proper widow should, Miss Mildred. Millen was gone. . . .

Christmas dinner moved to my house. Our families grew. Our children married and had children; each unit began staying home as it grew, establishing its own traditions. The coals from Bethlehem were shared for each hearth. The embers lived. Only Sister Sara, who has not yet been blessed with grandchildren, still eats with us and brings her brood.

Ever since the Bear Cat died, each year since Missa Pharaoh took over the family plot at Woolsey Baptist cemetery, I rise before day on Christmas morning and go there. I know them all. "Christmas gift," I say softly into the dawn, into the silence. And then I weep, as silently as the stones.

Last year on Christmas Eve I made a date. I invited two of my grandsons, Jimbo, who was eight, and Willie Fletch, who was six, to go with me on Christmas morning.

"For what?" they said.

"To get Christmas gift on the Bear Cat," I replied.

"Oh," said Willie Fletch. He paused. "Sure, I'll go." It was a foregone conclusion he would accept any invitation that included Jimbo.

"Christmas gift?" said Jimbo. "I know about that, Sambi; it drives me crazy. Daddy's always jumping out from some place scaring me to death and I can't ever get it on him, no matter how hard I try."

The sun was rising when I gathered them that morning, and it made the winter trees across the fields glow rose gold with slanted light. As we drew near Woolsey, our plans made, Jimbo spoke. "What are you going to do if he answers you, Sambi?"

Willie Fletch was attentively silent, but his eyes got bigger.

I did not laugh. "If that happens, Jimbo, it's every man for himself. I'll wait for you at the creek."

Willie Fletch's eyes returned to their normal size and he smiled.

"Well, I should think you'd like a chance to talk to him," Jimbo chided. "I would. I never knew him and I would sure like to visit with the Bear Cat for a while."

"He and I had lots of visits, Jimbo, and he would have loved you boys. Remember to slip up behind the big marker and remember not to step on graves."

We tiptoed. We bent over. We hugged the granite marker carved with "Sams. Compton. Giles. Cole." The boys looked at me and I nodded.

"Christmas gift!" they shrieked as they sprang around the sides and into the family plot.

"Christmas gift!" I yelled. Just as loud as I could.

The familiar tears started, but then the laughter came. "Christmas gift!" I exulted, and the boys echoed me.

On the way home in the car, I said, "Jimbo, will you do me a favor?"

"Depends on what it is."

"Would you sing 'Silent Night' for me?"

"Sure. I'll be glad to do that, Sambi."

And he did. In perfect pitch, key, tune, whatever words the people who know use to describe an absolutely beautiful and perfect moment in music. It was also a perfect moment in time.

The true meaning of Christmas.

Indeed.

Joy to the world, the Lord is come.

Let earth receive her King.

Let every heart prepare Him room

And Heaven and nature sing.

Yes. And more.

Christmas, they say, is for children. So, I think, is Christianity.

The Kingdom of Heaven is here.

The Kingdom of Heaven is within you.

Except ye become as a little child, ye shall not enter the Kingdom of Heaven.

Oh, Christmas gift! Christmas gift, everybody!

Ferrol Sams is the author of two best-selling novels, *Run with the Horsemen* and *The Whisper of the River*, and two collections of stories, *The Widow's Mite* and *The Passing*, both of which were regional bestsellers. A graduate of Mercer University and the Emory University School of Medicine, Sams lives in Fayetteville, Georgia, his family's home for generations. A practicing physician, he is currently Medical Director of the Fayette Medical Clinic.